I AM

Aspien*girl*®

The Unique Characteristics, Traits and Gifts of Females on the Autism Spectrum

By

Tania A. Marshall

I am AspienGirl®: The Unique Characteristics, Traits, and Gifts of Females on the Autism Spectrum.

Disclaimer
All the information, techniques, skills and concepts contained within this publication are of the nature of general comment only, and are not in any way recommended as individual advice. The intent is to offer a variety of information to provide a wider range of choices now and in the future, recognising that we all have widely diverse circumstances and viewpoints. Should any reader choose to make use of the information contained herein, this is their decision, and the author and publisher does not assume any responsibilities whatsoever under any conditions or circumstances. The author and publisher does not take responsibility for the results of the readers decision to use this information. It is recommended that the reader obtain their own independent advice.

Models are for illustrative purposes only, unless clearly stated otherwise.

Table of Contents

Dedication

To the warrior AspienGirls I have been privileged to work with over the years. Your stories encouraged me to write this book. You are all true heroes, able to use your unique combination of gifts and talents to overcome your challenges and limitations. Every day, you work in superhero drive to achieve what your peers can naturally do, with ease. You do not go unnoticed. You are not insignificant. You have what it takes to *Be Your Own Superhero* - the best version of yourself.

Introduction

AspienGirl®: \as-pee-en-ger-l\ ; AspienWoman :\ aspee-en-wo-man\

1. a young female from Planet Aspien®; an adult female from Planet Aspien®

2. a female with Asperger Syndrome; possessing similar and different characteristics than a male with Asperger Syndrome

3. a female with a differently wired brain

Over the years, I have worked with hundreds of females, of all ages, who have a stunning array of gifts and talents, in addition to challenges. This particular group of individuals all have the characteristic traits of Asperger Syndrome or High Functioning Autism. Many of them have discussed feeling different, alone, from another planet, or era, hence the term Planet Aspien®. The use of terms, for example "AspienGirl®" are used affectionately and serve as an identity for a group of females who feel isolated on populous planet Earth.

Many individuals have expressed an interest in a book such as this; from the individuals themselves to carers, parents, school personnel to professionals.

This book was written for three kinds of readers. First, I wrote this book for females, who themselves may identify with some or all of the characteristics; who may be self-diagnosed or formally diagnosed. Second, the book is for those that support females on the Spectrum; their family members, their carers, teachers or friends; and thirdly, for professionals (teachers, preschool staff, school counsellors, doctors, psychologists, psychiatrists, social workers, paediatricians), to become more familiar with the common, and at times subtle, presentations and to possibly aid in screening and better diagnostic processes.

I wrote this book to help spread awareness of this unique set of personality traits, preferences, characteristics, strengths, challenges and other traits. This book is the first in a series, designed to contribute to awareness and education. On each page, you will find *a quotation directly from an AspienGirl®* that illustrates a characteristic or trait, a photograph illustrating the trait and lastly, *a quotation from a parent, teacher, family member or professional*. Each picture has two different voices that both describe each characteristic and contribute to making a powerful visual description. Occasional quotes may be from AspienWomen reflecting on their younger years.

The traits in this book are not reflective of every person on the Spectrum and not every individual will have every characteristic listed. The words "aspie", "aspire", "autie", "aspiengirl", "aspienwoman", "aspergirl","asperwoman", and others are all terms used affectionately within the Autism Community.

Research on the Autistic female profile is very new, and as such, can be many years behind clinical and anecdotal observations. The female profile is a relatively new concept and field of research, and as such, many of the characteristics that are seen in clinics, inpatient and outpatient settings, schools, written about in blogs and books, have yet to be confirmed by solid research. There is a great need for research that focuses on the female profile and includes females on the Spectrum.

Whilst the DSM-5 now refers to the term Autism Spectrum Disorder, the term Asperger Syndrome is still used in every day communication, within the Autism community, and by some professionals, and is not likely to disappear, nor should it, for it would be a loss of identity in addition to ignoring the uniqueness of the Asperger profile. So, with this all in mind, please enjoy the visuals, quotes and sometime humorous look at this unique group of females, of which there are millions around the world, who can and do make significant contributions to humanity.

Acknowledgements

No book comes to fruition on its own. I would like to acknowledge the following people's contributions. This amazing group of females are trailblazers in their own right and I am most grateful to have their support. I would now like to acknowledge some extraordinary women who made it possible for this book to be read.

Dr Judith Gould, thank you for writing the Foreword to this book and for your invaluable knowledge, experience, expertise and feedback.

Dr Temple Grandin, thank you for reviewing my book and for shining your bright light wherever you go. I am most grateful to have your support in such an important endeavor and project.

Dr Shana Nichols, thank you for providing a testimonial for this book and for your important feedback, expertise, knowledge and insight.

Dr Jennifer Imig Huffman, thank you for your valuable advice and support. You are a diamond in the rough!

Thank you to all the girls, teens and their families, friends, carers and professionals for sharing their experiences and allowing me to showcase the unique characteristics, in their own words.

I would like to thank the amazing AspienGirl® Mentors Honey Parker and her mother Olley Edwards, Iris Grace and her mother Arabella, Lydia Tay and Maja Nilsson, for agreeing to showcase their talents and act as mentors of inspiration for other young females on the Spectrum.

I would like to thank the following people for perusing my drafts and providing me feedback: Dr Amanda Webster, Jeanette Purkis, Renee Salas and Julie Clark.

Last and certainly not least, I would like to thank Kylee Legge of the Publishing Queen (www.thepublishingqueen.com) for her professionalism, support, editing and assistance in this process.

Testimonials

I am Aspien Girl® is an exciting and timely book for girls on the spectrum! It is about time that the field of Autism pays attention to the needs of females on the spectrum and what a beautifully composed compilation of the unique female Autism experience.

For years, the field of Autism has been dominated by a focus on how the condition impacts boys. The research, assessments, diagnostic criteria and treatments were designed with a predominate bias toward the male model of Autism. Now it is time for the girls with Autism to have a voice. Females on the Autism spectrum do not develop or present with symptoms of Autism in the same ways as boys; however, the impact on their functioning is just as significant as it is for boys.

In her book, Tania Marshall raises the flag for awareness of females with Autism spectrum. She gives voice to the experiences of girls on the spectrum and their family members through a combination of exquisite pictures and beautiful quotes from children, families, and professionals who live and work with females on the spectrum.

For those impacted by Autism and for those who diagnose or treat this condition, this book is a must read and own. It will be an invaluable resource to educate professionals and families on the unique traits and gifts of girls on the spectrum. I plan to use it as an intro to Aspergers tool when I explain the diagnosis to parents. I'm excited to have this to show parents so they understand the symptoms and condition better.

For parents of girls on the spectrum, congratulations! You have in front of you an invaluable resource for educating your daughter on some of the more common traits of girls on the spectrum. As each child on the spectrum is different, I recommend sharing this book with your daughter and discussing with her the pages that remind her of herself and the ones that do not. This will help to recognise her unique experience and provide an opportunity to problem solve her areas of concern while highlighting her strengths and unique perspective.

Thank you Tania Marshall for giving a voice to females with Autism spectrum; their families, the children affected by this condition, and the field of Autism spectrum, particularly those who work with females on the spectrum, owe you a debt of gratitude.

Dr Jennifer Imig Huffman –
Parent and Professional

Where was this book when I was a child?! I related so very closely practically page-for-page. I even got a tear in my eye when I thought of the very lucky girls who will grow up being understood and appreciated. Priceless. This is a much-needed book and you hit the nail on the head. It's a book that makes you think. And it's a book written by a Professional extolling the positives and the gifts. Rare indeed! What a gem you've got on your hands!

Renee Salas –
Author of *Black and White: A colorful look at life on the Autism Spectrum*

I love the quotes throughout the book. They show a real life experience and remind the reader of your intense professional experience! Great idea.

Olley Edwards –
Director of the *Kindest Label* and Author of *Why Aren't Normal People Normal?*

This book is so beautiful; literally and figuratively. The colours and images are both pleasant and effective. The content brought so many memories of my own daughter's younger years back to life. It was as if someone stepped back in time and observed her. One thing this book does is emphasise the fact that many girls on the Autism Spectrum are empathetic creatures. So many do not believe "autism" and "empathy" can coexist in one individual. I assure you, they can. Also, each AspienGirl® is unique, and Tania does a fantastic job illustrating and underscoring that point. Some girls love to be a princess while others want anything but. Some are social, others are not. This book will challenge you to step away from the boys and view girls on the Autism Spectrum without distraction. They are unique beings who deserve to be understood in their own light. Thank you, Tania, for a practical yet sensitive resource for AspienGirls, their caregivers and professionals who support them.

Julie Clark –
Author of *Asperger's in Pink*

One of the brightest building blocks contributing to the emergence of a sisterhood of females on the Autism spectrum and those who support and love them. *I Am AspienGirl*® is a true gift to the community.

Dr Shana Nichols –
Clinical Psychologist and founder of ASPIRE Center for
Learning and Development in New York, USA
Leading Author of *Girls Growing Up on the Autism Spectrum*

An imaginative book with a positive message for girls with Autism or Aspergers.

Dr Temple Grandin –
Author of *The Autistic Brain*

Thank you so much for sending me your wonderful book. I think it is great, and fulfils a real need to raise awareness about women on the spectrum. There is an urgent need for more research with women and girls on the Autism spectrum. We don't yet know how much current diagnostic criteria and processes disadvantage females and whether those undiagnosed suffer in silence or manage to compensate effectively. Raising awareness of Autism spectrum conditions in females is an important first step, which this book achieves while reflecting the great diversity of experiences and opinions in this complex area.

Dr Francesca Happé, Professor of Cognitive Neuroscience, Director & Head of Department,
President, International Society for Autism Research (INSAR), MRC Social, Genetic &
Developmental Psychiatry Centre, UK

I just looked through your wonderful book. It is excellent! I think it adds a lot of value to the available information on girls and Autism. I think that parents of girl Aspies and Auties will find it very helpful (and probably girl Aspies and Auties themselves will too!). Through quotes from AspienGirls and their families, teachers and carers, artworks and imagery, *I am AspienGirl*® paints a vibrant picture of what life is like for girls with Asperger Syndrome. The book focuses on the often overlooked and misunderstood female profile of Asperger Syndrome and Autism. This book will be of interest to parents of AspienGirls, clinicians working with them and girls or women with Asperger Syndrome themselves. This is an accessible and valuable addition to the literature on Autism.

Jeanette Purkis –
Author of *The Wonderful World of Work: A Workbook for Asperteens*

Foreword

Dr Judith Gould

Consultant Clinical Psychologist and Director of the NAS Lorna Wing Centre for Autism, UK

The term AspienGirl®, as the title of Tania Marshall's book is very appropriate and reflects what girls in the Autism spectrum often say: that they feel they are from a different planet.

The rationale for this book is to address awareness of females with Autism or Asperger Syndrome who are often misdiagnosed and receive inappropriate interventions or who are simply not diagnosed. The book also emphasises advocacy for this group with their unique needs and challenges, education about the female profile and the differences between males and females.

For professionals working in this fascinating field the comments and statements of the girls and their parents are illuminating, clever and often funny. They highlight the obvious and not so obvious subtle differences in the way Autism is manifested in females. This has special significance when considering a diagnosis. The core difficulties in Autism are the same for all individuals within the spectrum but there are gender differences and it is the way these behaviours are manifested and interpreted that is important. Many clinicians/diagnosticians still have a male stereotype of what behaviours constitute Autism and dismiss girls and women because they do not fit this rigid, narrow view. It is now time for change and the examples given in this book constitute a major step forward in re-thinking the diagnosis of females on the spectrum.

The emphasis throughout the book highlights the strengths and positive attributes of the females but their 'difference' has to be acknowledged by everyone living and working with them. A sympathetic 'mentor' in the education system can make or break a young girl's future. As professionals we need to be informed about the way young women think and perceive the world. This book gives us this insight. Tania Marshall's way of describing the strengths and pitfalls for females on the spectrum using pictures and photographs is much more meaningful than words alone. These visual presentations will give guidance to professionals when explaining the diagnosis as this type of presentation makes more sense to a girl on the spectrum.

The book is divided into sections with delightful visual presentations covering all aspects of daily life, play, social interaction, language and communication, sensory and emotional needs, together with strengths and challenges in all these areas.

Five important needs of AspienGirls are highlighted which remind us of the uniqueness of each individual and how we as professionals and parents should accommodate them. The appendices give further useful information on commonly observed traits and characteristics of girls, how the book can be utilized by parents, carers, professionals, teachers and educational staff, "Aspiengirl Mentor" and "What I like about me" activity sheets, gender differences from both research based information and clinical observation, and lastly, Tania's future projects.

A final quote from a girl on the spectrum. "With the diagnosis and the right support we Aspien Girls have been known to soar..."

This book is a must for everyone living and working with girls on the Autism spectrum.

I AM Aspien*girl*®   17

I am a girl with Asperger Syndrome or High Functioning Autism, an AspienGirl®. I was told I am unique, have many strengths and some challenges.

In our research, we have learnt that there are many more females on the Autism Spectrum than previously thought and that the gender statistics are more likely closer to 2:1 (males to females).

– Mother of 6-year-old

They said my brain is wired differently from most other people, and that I was born this way.

She had this amazing array of super-abilities from very early on. She started to speak articulately and in sentences from the age of 18 months.
– Father of 4-year-old

People often said I was "different", "odd", or "unique" from early on. I assumed everyone thought like me.

I always knew something was different about her from very early on, not anything bad ... she is amazing, she is different, unique, eccentric, intuitive and highly sensitive. She is often described by others as an 'old soul' and I'm often told she has been here before. People have referred to her as odd and once she was described as from another planet ... she even has a dialect of her own!   – Parent

I was often bored and wondered if I was adopted. I even asked my mum that once. I asked her all kinds of questions.

She never wanted to do what we were doing. She was off pretending to be animals, fairies, unicorns, or superheroes of some kind, and she constantly asked me questions.   – Mother of 5-year-old

I was told I was reading chapter books before I had started school. They called it Hyperlexia.

I remember that she talked and read quite early on and tended to take things literally. We would say, "Look sweetie, we're home." She would say, "No we are not, we are in the driveway!" Also, once at the zoo, we said to her "Look honey, it's a dinosaur". She replied with, "No it's not, that's a Triceratops!" She was two years old then. That's when we decided we were going to find a psychologist that understood her."

– Mother and Father

My dad told me I was an out-of-the-box thinker and I remember asking him, "What box?!" I loved cardboard boxes!

I could never think of the ideas she comes up with. She is mostly anti-conformist and very creative. One time I told her that her imagination was running away with her and she said, "My imagination does not know how to run!"
– Teacher of 10-year-old

Our mother told us we are both AspienGirls, but we arc different from each other.

I have three girls, all on the Spectrum and each is one different. The twins are a Tomboy and a Princess. My teen Aspien is a total Bookworm.
– Mother of three

I was often called the "Little Philosopher". At school and at home for a long time it was remarked upon that I was 'away with the fairies' as I was a daydreamer. Mum would often say "Earth to Lynda" and it was a source of amusement along with my 'lack of common sense' and my constant asking of questions.

It's like a tsunami of information coming at her. She says she cannot keep up with her brain. She is an introverted deep thinker. She craves knowledge and I really struggle to keep up with her.
— Father of 8-year-old

They tell me I worry too much and I need to just go and play.

A large part of my professional work involves teaching girls how to think in more helpful ways. It's a very important life skill.
– Developmental/educational psychologist

I have never been able to sleep very well because my brain doesn't want to go to sleep.

She wants to go to sleep but she says her brain keeps talking to itself. Just last night she said, "Mummy, my brain told me a story". She really seems to have these nocturnal-like kind of hours, especially when it's a full moon.   – Mother

Mum says I am 5 going on 30. She says that means I am not concerned about the same things that other girls my age are.

My daughter often seems like she is an adult, having missed childhood altogether.
– Mother

My head is so full it often hurts.

She has been diagnosed with Asperger Syndrome, giftedness and learning difficulties. She often says she wishes her brain had an 'off' button. She is just like her aunt. They said it was hereditary. She won't let them or us help her. She needs to learn to ask for help.   – Parents

I hate making mistakes.
Why can't I get it the first time?

She is perfectionistic and way too
harsh and critical of herself.
– Uncle

TANIA A. MARSHALL

My parents think I need to see a psychologist. I told them I'm not going to see yet another shrink who isn't going to help me.

She is very strong-willed and is not motivated by her peers' opinions, although now as a teenager she appears to be quite aware of her peers' perceptions. She has transitioned through many stages in search for an identity. She refuses to see another psychologist who doesn't understand the unique perspective of girls on the spectrum.   – Mother

I love working on my own and doing my own thing.

She just thrives in one-on-one situations, or when she is presenting to others. She has worked hard. She is now a professional actress, but I say she's been acting all her life!

– Mother of adult actress with Aspergers

By age 7 I had mastered the art of blending in with the walls. I began to enjoy school, I loved learning and I did well academically. It was exhausting and I would retreat to my room and play alone when I got home.

She is often off with the fairies. We took her to the doctor for a hearing test, but they said she was fine. She lives in her own fantastical world, Kylie-Land, an alternate reality, where time, reality, and rules are set by her. It can be frustrating for us. For her, it seems that the best world is the one inside her head. It is so interesting, and wonderfully complicated in there. – Parents of 9-year-old

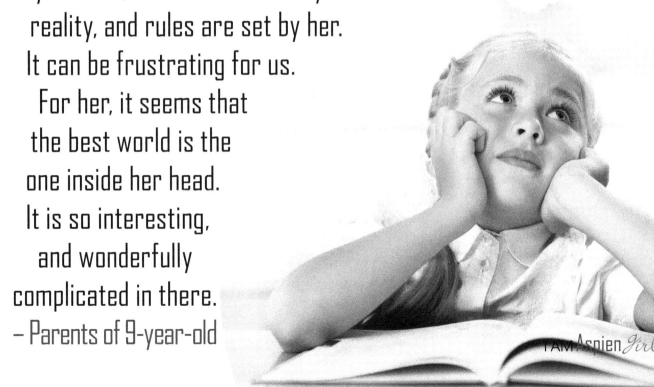

One of my challenges is reading comprehension.

She has Irlen Syndrome, a genetic visual perceptual dyslexia, also known as Scotopic Sensitivity System (SSS). Her grandmother and I also have this Syndrome.
— Mother

She is "different", has some uneven skills and seems to prefer to teach herself the material, rather than be taught by me. She has an advanced reading ability and Dyscalculia, difficulty in learning or comprehending arithmetic. – Teacher

The teacher said she is passive, quiet, and at times, appears to lack interest in classroom activities. She often gets accolades and certificates for good behaviour at school and tends to hang out in the library during lunchtime.

– Mother

I have one friend who is my best friend and I am happy.

She only has one friend in school and I worry what will happen if he moves away. She gets upset when he plays with others and tells me, "But he said he was MY best friend!" She just doesn't see any need to have more friends.   – Classroom teacher

They tell me I'm smart, but some of my grades are terrible.

my brain hurts **MIDTERMS!!** sigh...... *my teacher must hate me*

i cant do this When will i ever need to use the periodic table in real life? **why me???**

IM STRESSING **ALGERBRA GUAHHH** SCHOOL IS KILLING ME HOMEWORK GIVES ME A HEADACHE

IS IT SUMMER VACATION YET? **HELP!!** IM HAVING A CRISIS

I DONT GET IT .....REALLY REALLY CONFUSED ID RATHER BE TEXTING **BORINGGGGG**

EXAMS SERIOUSLY ALL THIS READING CAN NOT BE GOOD FOR MY EYES (I LIKE GUM...i like gum A LOT. i really really REALLYYY I WISH I HAD A PIECE OF GUM) **300 word essay**

I JUST WANNA SLEEP BORING IM GONNA HAVE A BREAKDOWN...NO 4 REAL CONFUSING

THIS IS UNFAIR **I WANNA BE LEFT ALONE**

QUIZ *GETTING A MIGRAINE* **misunderstood**

IM SLEEPY **UGHHHH** IM NEVER GONNA BE DONE

SIGHHHHHHHH..

Read Chapters and 5, then (BLAHHH BLAHHH) answer questions (blahh..)

She is like the absent-minded professor. We can find her by following the pile of belongings up the hallway; backpack, jumper, shoes, socks, water bottle. How can she be so bright in Science and Computers, yet so messy and disorganised? — Parents

Why do I have homework? I just spent all day at school!

Every night it's the same fight ... to get her to do her homework ... she says school is school and home is home. She is a perfectionist.

– Parents

TANIA A. MARSHALL

They are always talking in class. I can hear them whispering and I can't concentrate. I love learning, especially English literature and art.

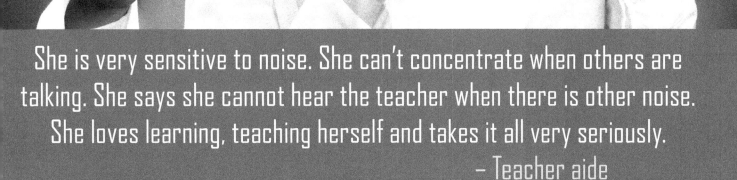

She is very sensitive to noise. She can't concentrate when others are talking. She says she cannot hear the teacher when there is other noise. She loves learning, teaching herself and takes it all very seriously.

– Teacher aide

My best friend is David. He is so much fun to play with.
I prefer to play with the boys rather than the girls sometimes,
because girls can be confusing to me.

She prefers intense single friendships.   – Grandmother of 6-year-old

I try really hard to be good and fit in. I have no idea why the other kids don't like me.

She does try really hard. Early on we could see that she could observe, copy, mimic or imitate, in order to fit in socially. We saw it as a protective mask that we knew she needed to wear around groups of people. She seems to prefer playing with younger or older people.
– Parents

Mum says I need to make more friends.

She is often on the outer of the group and only when comfortable will she then join in with her peers. She just doesn't seem to get what to do socially.

– Mother of 6-year-old girl

People sometimes say I am a "tattletale" and I need to mind my own business.

She says she is not bossy, that she just knows what we should be doing! She is a little director often telling people what to do and moralising to anyone who will listen. The irony is she hates being told what to do herself!

– Teacher

I don't know why I get in trouble sometimes ... but my brother and sisters just don't do the right thing ...

Her ability to direct others and be on rule patrol gets her in trouble at times ... She really benefited from a social group where she learned and practised social skills.
– Parents of a family of 5, with 3 children on the Spectrum

It took me a while to understand that her opposition was partly due to not understanding the social hierarchy, social boundaries, group roles ... I soon learned that using logic and reasoning in explaining my requests worked well. She finds it challenging to have to listen to others ... and she likes to think she's my boss!

– Mother of teenage girl

I'm always in trouble ... but Mum is just so confusing ... she doesn't mean what she says or say what she means.

I'm not so good at some things, but you know what? Creativity is about getting messy, and I am very creative!

Despite her superpower strengths, she just can't seem to get organised, find what she is looking for, manage her time or plan ahead.

– A stressed-out mother

TANIA A. MARSHALL

I AM Aspien *girl*

I liked categorising my books with index cards using my typewriter and playing librarian. Yeah, I did that … super geeky like …

My daughter was heartbroken when she finished reading the 6th instalment of her favourite book series. She was so distressed that she wrote the 7th book on her own. Her psychologist told her to send it to the author! She loves writing, has a blog and says she is going to be an author one day.   – Mother of 10-year-old

Homeschooling has been the best for me where I am free to be who I am.

She was a square peg in a round hole and just did not fit in at school. She would often talk to me late at night about her feelings of not fitting in. Everything comes out about her day at that time and I feel blessed that she can share with me.

– A grateful mum who gets to see her daughter's confidence grow in herself day by day.

I made some friends although as usual always felt odd and like I didn't quite fit in.

She can make eye contact and socialise for short periods of time. She uses social echolalia.   – Psychologist

I couldn't figure out why she would be so tired after a social event. She can socialise quite well in small doses … just not as long as her peers can. Her social "cup" fills up very quickly.   – Parents

I like playing with my friends, but I get so tired.

Family functions and holidays are particularly challenging. Without adequate time alone, she feels completely worn out and suffers from a "social hangover".   – Parent

I would watch and listen to them play and talk. I tried very hard to figure out what they were doing and why they were doing it, but it didn't make a lot of sense to me.

From very early on we noticed her watching others. She collects information about people, observing them, like studying them, learning about them.
We called her the people watcher.   – Father

I have some trouble keeping friends, sometimes say the wrong thing and am bothered by things that don't bother other kids.

She wants to interact, but she doesn't know how. She often mimics others around her like she is wearing different masks. She copies and imitates her friends, books, comics and TV shows. We're starting to not know who she is anymore. She's a bit of a Chameleon.   – Parents

I have trouble understanding body language. I have read and studied body language books, often practising in the mirror.

She is really trying – unsuccessfully – to fit in by being ultra-feminine. We just don't know how to help her. She is 'sensitive' to standing out, is desperate to fit in but doesn't know how to do it. It seems that when God made her, He gave her an extra sprinkle of intelligence and a little less sprinkle in social understanding.

– Mother of teenager

Thinking back, during my adolescence I felt like I was a hostage on an alien planet that has totally screwed up social rules.

She recently has given up trying to fit in. She is going through very challenging teenage years, feeling even more of an outcast. We are now watching her embrace opposite conventions, despise femininity, social and gender rules. She is now a tomboy and a bit confused about her gender.   – Parents

They are always saying I'm the ringleader. Ringleader? I'm just struggling to fit in somewhere ... Anywhere.

She went from princess, to tomboy, to punk to emo to goth. She is having trouble finding out just who she is and has gotten involved with the wrong types of people. She is not interested in dating and finds flirting very confusing. She also does not seem to have a solid gender identity.
– Confused Parents of AspienTeen

In hindsight, the loneliest and most confusing time was in my teen years.

We all thought she had gone to the "dark side". She just didn't fit in anywhere and had no idea of who she was. She seemed to despise femininity and defied social and gender rules. When she has friends, she tends to naively and blindly follow wherever they go; their rules, taking on their traits, from the way they dress to the way they talk and act. She would overapologise and repeat "Are you ok?" over and over again. It was then we realized she was having trouble reading others' non-verbal signals.   – Parents

I love teaching. I am going to be a teacher when I grow up.

She dresses up her toys, teddy bears, the dog, her brother, anyone who will listen! Her lessons were always 'above' the level of her friends. She has a lot of imaginary friends and animals.

– Older sister of 10-year-old

I love my animals, stationery items, toy ponies, rocks, frogs and insects.

She collects ... no ... she hoards, crystals and rocks ... I couldn't understand why my bag was so heavy and found she had filled it full of rocks. She had taken some from her psychologists office! She is fascinated by water – dams, creeks, swamps, waterfalls, the beach. She would spend hours at the river playing by herself, if she could.

– Aunt of 4-year-old

I love my toy house. Mum says I have to let others play with it too, but they touch my toys and I don't like it when they move things out of place.

Her play is one of ordering, organising, categorising and grouping ... she has collected and knows all the names of the Littlest Pet Shop animals, their ages, their breeds ... She spends her time setting up toys, preferring order, symmetry or groups.

– Psychologist

I love animals ... they are my best friends.

She was always role-playing the doctor ... now she is in University studying to become a vet!   – Father

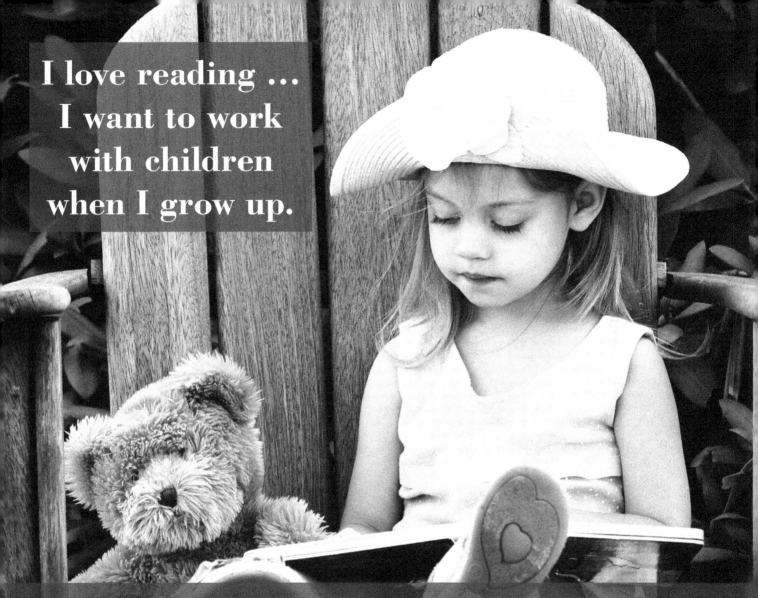

I love reading ...
I want to work
with children
when I grow up.

She loved to spend her time role-playing the class teacher. We think
she could be a great school principal.
– Aunt of 9-year-old

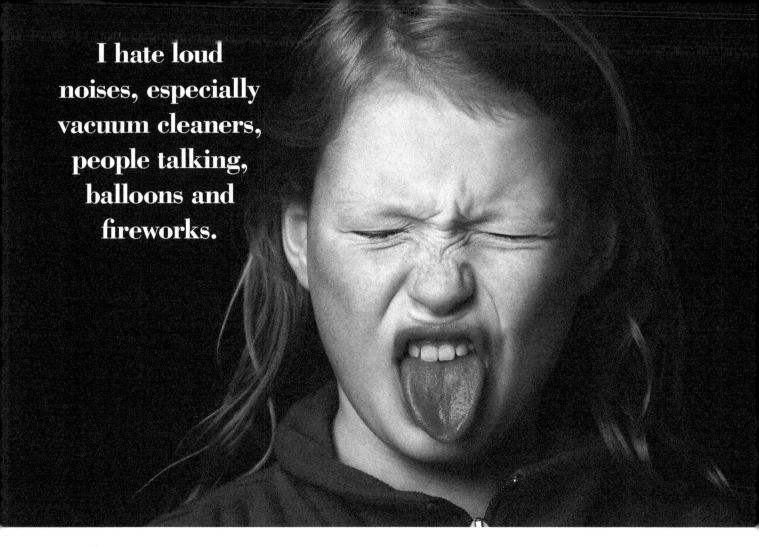

I hate loud noises, especially vacuum cleaners, people talking, balloons and fireworks.

She refuses to brush her teeth, let me brush her hair, touch her head and is picky with her food. Loud or sudden noises overwhelm her. A burst balloon is her worst-ever nightmare.

– Mother of 7-year-old

Mum says I am a picky eater and I have never been able to swallow pills. They make me gag.

It has been a fight from day one to get her to eat. She won't take any medication and now is quite thin. I am worried she may have an eating disorder.   – Aunt

I was very competitive and perfectionistic, in everything, even when I had no one really to compete with.

I believe AspienGirls are warriors because they fight battles – big sensory, emotional, communication and social battles, on a daily basis. They really do dance to the beat of a different drum.
– Special needs teacher

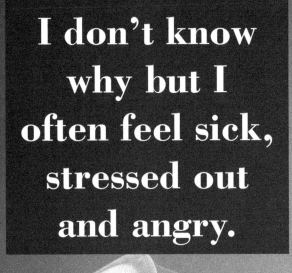

I don't know why but I often feel sick, stressed out and angry.

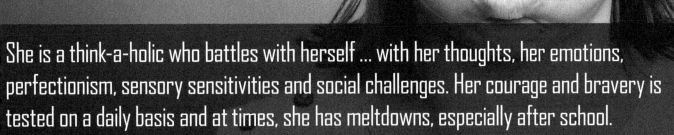

She is a think-a-holic who battles with herself ... with her thoughts, her emotions, perfectionism, sensory sensitivities and social challenges. Her courage and bravery is tested on a daily basis and at times, she has meltdowns, especially after school.

– Father

I don't like being touched or hugged, or clothing tags, they feel like razors.

She hates it when people assume that she wants to be cuddled. Our extended family She was just diagnosed with Sensory Processing Disorder. Loud noises, bright lights Her psychologist helped us put together a sensory management kit for her and it has touch with calming music and apps to help her to stay calm or calm down, a small fidget toy, her favourite stuffed toy and a small ultra-soft blanket. This bag is with

members don't understand this and think she is quite rude.
and people touching her are really distressing for her.
really helped. Her kit has ear-plugs, head-phones, her iPod
bottle with her favourite essential oil, a hat and sunglasses, a
her 24/7 and it has improved things a lot.   – Mother

I bump and crash into things a lot.

She can trip on air. In our family we joke around saying that "the furniture is out to get her and the floor bullies her." She recently broke her leg, just falling on it the wrong way. We were told we needed to take her to an Occupational Therapist who then diagnosed her with Developmental Co-ordination Disorder. We thought she was just a bit clumsy. We had no idea.   – Parents

She loves her rocking horse, swings and hammock. She will spent hours just swinging.

She sometimes sways when stressed, grinds or clenches her teeth, twirls her hair or bites her nails. She now has a stress ball and some chewellery, which she has with her all the time. This helps her to achieve a calmer state. It is called "self-soothing".
– Developmental/Educational Psychologist

I just seem to know stuff about people.

She was always telling us things about family members or other people that she couldn't possibly know ... even things about the people who used to live in the house before us ... it was spooky ... we would do some research and you know what? She was right every time!   – Mother

People say I am too serious. Mum told me I was even a serious baby.

She reacts to the world with much intensity and has always found it a challenge to relax. – Mother

They say I'm too sensitive, too emotional and that I care too much. How can you care too much?

She is very sensitive and caring. She can feel hurt or moved by scenes in movies that do not give her siblings the same feelings. We have to monitor what she watches. She is a little Diva and I love it. That's just her.   – Mother of 5-year-old

At one stage, I would tell my Mum that I was going back to my Nanna's whenever I got in trouble.

Urgent! Seeking new family who will let me have MY way!

She has a bag packed under her bed and whenever things don't go her way, she goes out to the road ... she can be very dramatic and over the top.   – Mother

They always tell me to smile for a photo, but I just don't understand why I should.

At times, she is emotionally too honest. She tends to show exactly how she feels about someone in front of them and that has not bode too well for her.   – Teacher

TANIA A. MARSHALL

They are always asking me if I'm upset, but I'm just thinking!

She often doesn't know how to show her true feelings on her face and we incorrectly assume she is bored, serious or angry. But when asked, she simply replies that she is thinking. That is her "resting face".   – Grandmother

I AM Aspien *girl*®   75

I get in trouble sometimes for laughing when I am supposed to be serious ...

Recently, she was disrespectful and her father told her so. He was very stern and she burst into laughter. He believes that she did that on purpose, but I honestly don't think she understands that laughing was inappropriate.

– Mother

Sometimes I don't know how to talk about my feelings. I can get them all mixed up. It's confusing.

She has been diagnosed with Alexithymia. She needs help with expressing, understanding and describing her experience of emotions and those of other people.
– Autism Specialist

> ## I remember crying and crying and crying ... I don't know why.

Most days she is so tired after school, and wants to be alone. I'm sure her teacher thinks I'm nuts when I explain the hour-long meltdowns at home. She lets out all that has built up inside her during the day. Basically, she explodes. It isn't aimed at anyone, but it leaves us completely bewildered.

– Family members

They call me a Diva.

She is easily offended, yet she dishes out twice as much to the others ... at times making a mountain out of a molehill. She tends not to get jokes, misinterprets others' intentions and burns bridges.

– Parents

"Some people think that because I have Autism it means that I don't have feelings for others, however, I feel others' emotions too strongly. It is overwhelming to me"

She can walk into a room and feel what everyone is feeling. The problem is that it all comes in faster than she can process it. She feels too much. She is often told she is too sensitive, too emotional and she needs to toughen up. Her mother can barely get her to go to school.
– Psychologist/Autism specialist

They say I care too much ... am too sensitive ... they say I have the world on my shoulders ... don't they know that's impossible?!

She is so serious ... about saving the world, the rules and justice ... often helping too much and doing too much for others ... she is now studying to be an environmental lawyer and that career is just perfect for her.

– Mother

They say I'm intense, moody, that I over-react, I'm a drama queen, too emotional ...

She has always experienced strong emotions. Yes, she cries easily, because she is very sensitive and gets easily hurt. Her psychologist has mentioned she might be bi-polar, as bipolar and Autism spectrum can overlap.

– Aunt of teenager

I really don't like it when people look at me. It makes me feel like I am naked.

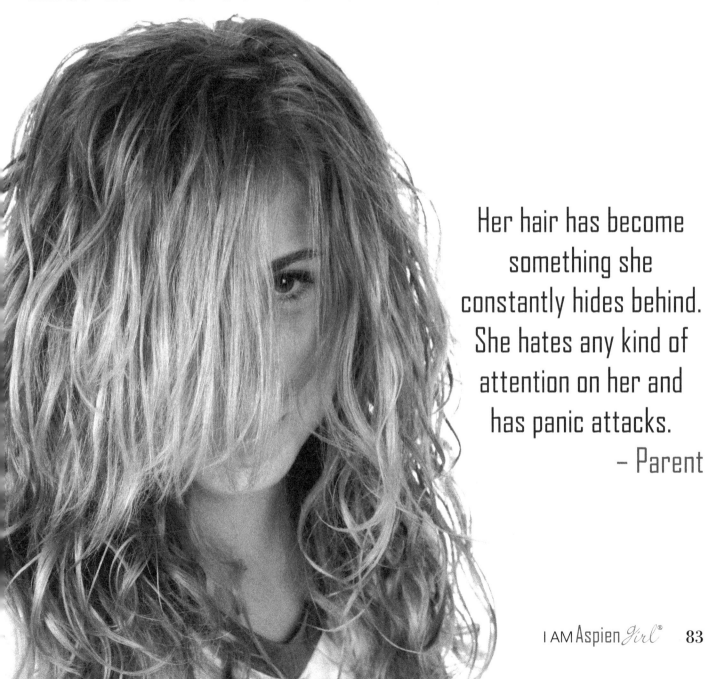

Her hair has become something she constantly hides behind. She hates any kind of attention on her and has panic attacks.

– Parent

The world doesn't care enough … someone needs to stand up for the rights of animals.

At times she catastrophises, blowing the smallest issue right out of proportion. She is now a vegetarian, has always had high sense of justice and is an animal rights activist
– Father of teenage Aspien

I often get told I need to dress more conservatively, but that's so boring.

She did some strange things as a teenager. She embraced a variety of alternative lifestyles, much to the distress of the family. She has always had her own sense of "style". She is now a famous tattoo artist. People come from all over for her work.
– Foster Mother

I hate my life. Being a teenager sucks. The only thing that keeps me sane is my bass guitar.

Just a few months ago she was wearing frilly dresses and looked like a princess. Now, she's Goth and won't let anyone call her by her real name. She has depression and panic attacks that sneak up on her from out of nowhere
– Horrified Parents

I have always struggled to fit in and I got depressed in my teenage years. I have fought my way out ... over and over again.

She really struggles with sensory sensitivities, social anxiety, panic attacks and depression. She must have gone through at least three or four different lifestyle changes.

— Parents

There are times I am so terrified and I can't talk ... they say I'm shy.

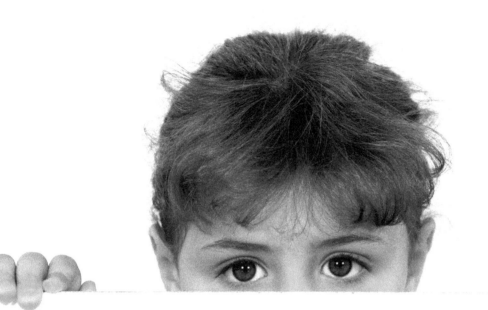

She is introverted ... quiet, shy ... socially anxious ... intensely private, at times mute. This is the exact opposite of most of her peers at her school ... she flies under the radar because she is so well-behaved.

— Guidance Officer

When they were passing out the 'girly' genes in Heaven, I was definitely at the end of the line. I thought boys were stupid too. I didn't get why when boys pushed you down on the playground or stepped on you, it meant he liked you.

She even has a T-shirt that says "I hate everybody".
– Mother of teenage Aspien

People keep telling me to stay quiet and that I talk too much. I was extremely talkative and was nicknamed 'chatterbox'.

She is on talk overload most of the time and often has a real need to tell me everything. She often has challenges with others because of this. She has always had an advanced vocabulary and her constantly correcting other people's errors gets her into trouble.

– Mother

I love big books and I read as much as I can.

It's a real challenge for her to keep her mind on schoolwork. I often find her absorbed in books ...

— Mother of tween girl

I read Harry Potter in Maths class most of last year ... my teacher didn't even notice.

She reads them like we breathe air. No, she doesn't just read them; she climbs inside the book and lives there. – Father of tween girl

I love anime, languages and K-pop.

We are of Caucasion English background yet she is obsessed with Korean pop music, languages and Asian cultures. She knows Japanese and is now teaching herself Korean. She watches her K-pop on YouTube over and over and over again

— Confused father.

Mum made me a Medieval princess costume which I considered to be an 'exact' replica of a dress of the era for a fancy dress party at Brownies. I was very upset that a girl in a decorated cardboard box won the prize.

She has always been fascinated with the Victorian era. She writes all sorts of stories using quite formal Victorian-esque vocabulary. She brushes her hair 100 times before bed every night and she begs me to put her hair in rags to give her Victorian ringlets!
– Exasperated mother of tween living in the Victorian Era

I'm not sure whether I want to fly a plane or build one.

She has always been fascinated with physics, flight and machines that fly. She knows all about Amelia Earhart – Grandfather, Pilot and Aviator

I love butterflies, fairies, unicorns, angels, dragons and elves.

Her head-world is all of her own design. It is fantasy ... books, fairies, unicorns, princesses, mermaids, animals, nature ... just to name a few.
— Grandmother

I set up my 'Unicorn Club' and made badges that my sister and her friend had to wear. Club membership dwindled to one ... me.

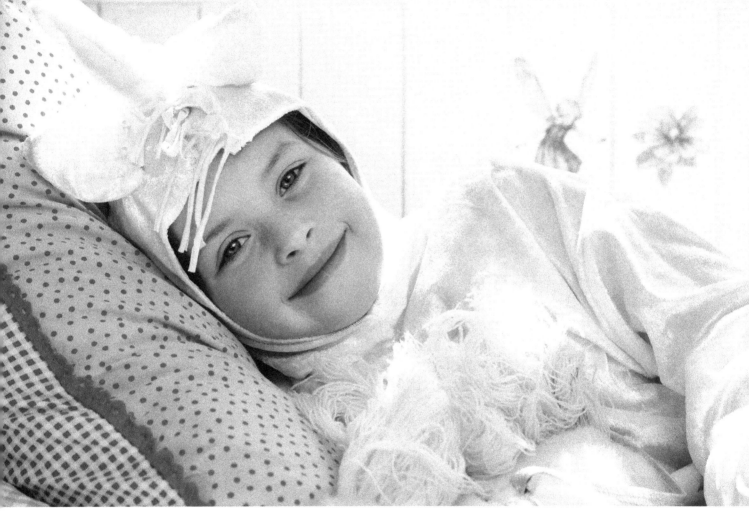

She often blends fantasy in with reality, and this is confusing for us all.
– Grandmother

I love animals.
Thula is my best friend.

www.irisgracepainting.com

My daughter works at a large zoo with the animals. She loves her job and has a natural affinity with the animals.
– Parent of 30-year-old

I asked for another cat, but Mum says one is enough.

She is inseparable from her cat. When she was younger, we even had to set the table for Sparkle at dinnertime.   – Parent

I love cuddling my dog.
She makes me feel better.

She has never come to me for a hug. She gets comfort from her pets or teddy bears, rather than us. We did take it personally for awhile.

– Mother

Animals are my best friends.

I think she finds it much easier to understand and connect with animals. She is with them as much as she can. She even sleeps with them.

– Parent

I have my very own 'Smart Pup', who keeps me safe and helps me.

www.smartpups.org.au

We have a Smart Pup, a task-specific Assistance Dog trained to help our daughter with handling day-to-day routines and events. I can't tell people enough about the difference that this dog has had on our daughter's life, and our lives.   – Parents

Rainbow Summer is my BFF...

She is crazy about her horse. They have this surreal connection.   – Parents

I love water
and insects ...
and trees.

She has this profound
connection to nature.
She is an aesthete, at
one with the natural
environment, having a
profound connection and
deep sensitivity for art,
beauty and nature. She
gets upset when people
kill a fly.
— Grandmother

As a teenage I got lost in *Gladiator* and *Lord of the Rings*. I wrote out the scripts and rewrote things to include myself as one of the characters. I'd look forward to getting home so I could have these things on in the background. I was an elf and I would have imaginary conversations all the time.

We bought her all the movies and books in the series, the doll characters, clothing, costumes and elvish jewellery. She wore Arwen's Evenstar necklace 24/7. We think that she thinks she really is from Rivendell.   – Father

I am really good at some things ... my psychologist told me I have "Aspienpowers".

Before her diagnosis she used up all her energy trying to fit in. Since her diagnosis, she has bloomed and I am so proud of her. She has worked very hard – like a warrior does. We now focus on guiding her in the direction of her strengths while supporting her weaknesses.   – Mother of 10-year-old

Like ... Aspienpower Intelligence ... I have average to genius intelligence.

> We spent a lot on money on assessment and diagnosis and it was really worth it. We found out she has Aspergers, is really smart and has a unique profile of strengths and some weaknesses. We also found out what type of learner she is and how best to teach her.
> – Happy and relieved parents

Aspienpower Creativity and Imagination ...
I love painting ... it's my favourite thing to do.

www.irisgracepainting.com

Iris has been painting for quite a while now. She is now 4 years old and mostly non-verbal. We have made a website for her and sell her paintings.   – Mother

Aspienpower Hyperempathy...
I heard Mum say I need to stop bringing animals and people home.

She has brought home injured birds, dogs and cats ... even homeless people. We cannot afford the vet bills and she doesn't understand why we are unhappy when she brings home her homeless friends. Her naivety is astounding and she doesn't understand the context of the situation. She feels the emotions of animals and humans intensely. At times, we think she has too much empathy. She sees the person's need first, not the homelessness, mental illness, or drug addiction.

– Parents

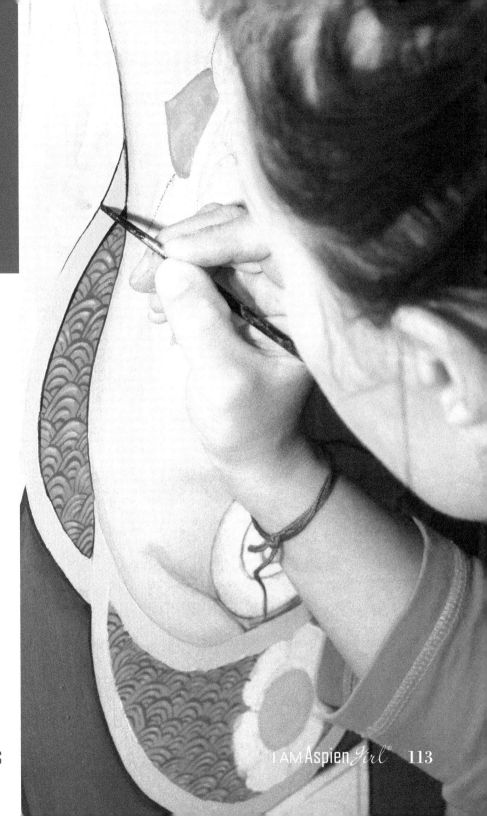

> **Art is the only thing I am interested in. My parents say they love my artwork, so what's the problem?**

She has this laser Aspienpower hyperfocus, where she loves being in the Asperzone, content to be by herself with her animals, computer, or books. Never mind that she would sit and draw for hours on end, or that she had a rich fantasy world with characters she gave names and voices to. She spends hours and hours doing what she loves. We have to remind her to eat, drink and go to the bathroom.

– Parents

Aspienpower self-taught.

I have seen her teach herself to play an instrument (she cannot read music to save herself) or teach herself a variety of dance genres and then teach others. It's remarkable. She is exceptionally good at anything she sets her mind to.   – Parent

Aspienpower sense of humour ...

She is so funny that we are helping her with acting lessons so she can pursue being a comedian, like me.
– Uncle and professional comedian

Aspienpower
Determination
I will fly! I will fly one day ...

She has a "strong will" and "limitless determination" to achieve what she sets her mind on, and occasionally her will is to her detriment.
– Special needs teacher

5 Important AspienGirl® needs
by Tania A. Marshall

1. Let me come out of the box.

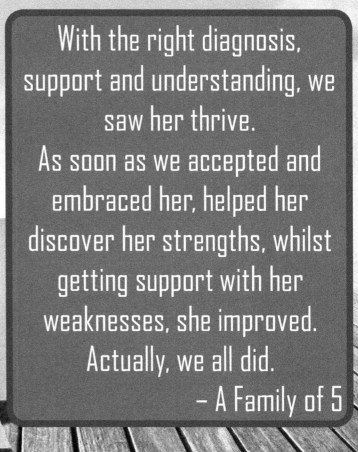

With the right diagnosis, support and understanding, we saw her thrive.
As soon as we accepted and embraced her, helped her discover her strengths, whilst getting support with her weaknesses, she improved. Actually, we all did.

— A Family of 5

2. Give me space and solitude ... it takes me a lot of energy to keep up socially.

Giving her breaks of solitude at home, at school, at any social event will help her to restore her emotions and recharge her battery.
— Psychologist

TANIA A. MARSHALL

3. Accept and love me unconditionally. Focus on what I can do and try to learn more about me.

At times, it is challenging for us but we love her unconditionally.
– Parents

4. Help me to learn about by emotions and how to manage them on my own. Provide me direct instruction about nonverbal communication, facial expressions, appropriate distance and boundaries, body language, mind-reading, and conversational skills, to help support me at home and school.

Our psychologist taught her (and us) about degrees of emotions, body clues, triggers, non-verbal body language and self-regulation. She has saved our family from what was once a terrifying place to be.

– Grateful parents

5. Help me discover and pursue my strengths, gifts and talents.

I have not met a female on the Spectrum that does not have gifts. They can spend hours focused on their subject matter, draw in very fine detail, write stories, learn anything they want to learn, be self-taught or practise their music over and over again. They often do not eat or drink, move or to go to the toilet, so they need to learn to take breaks.   – Psychologist.

We assure you, we're worth it, with a diagnosis and the right support we AspienGirls have been known to fly; we can be our own superheroes.

Early intervention was remarkable. Although the journey has been challenging at times, she is just absolutely soaring now.
– Parents

Real life true Aspien superheroes.

"It was when she finally dropped the fake smile and discovered and pursued her gifts that we saw her fly".

I have never seen her happier, less confused and more productive since the diagnosis and support.   – Parents

I am AspienGirl®. I am Maja Nilsson and I am 17 years old. I am a musician.

I am AspienGirl®. I am Honey Parker and I am 12 years old.

I am an actress.

I am AspienGirl®. I am Lydia Tay and I am 19 years old. I am a musician.

Appendix 1

Some Commonly Observed Characteristics and Traits of Young AspienGirls and AspienTeens

Disclaimer: This is not a diagnostic test. Please take this detailed list to a professional who preferably has some knowledge of or specialises in female Autism/Aspergers, if you or someone you know identifies with the majority of traits. This table is based on clinic experiences, observations, anecdotal evidence, and descriptions by others. There is a great need for female-based research. Autism tends to be a *condition of extremes*; hence, for example girls tend to be either superior with or disabled by mathematics. It is also important to remember that Autism is a heterogeneous condition.

Emotional
Experiences intense rapid emotions, particularly bursts of anxiety, panic and anger
Has difficulty controlling her emotions, experiences generalised anxiety and/or has OCD
Meltdowns tend to be caused by emotional overload, sensory overload, social overload, being a highly sensitive child and/or information overload
Emotionally immature compared to her peers
A tendency to cry when frustrated, angry, and/or anxious
More likely to internalise, may be mute and/or shy
Tend to be described as sensitive, shy, anxious, depressive, passive or avoidant
May have an anxiety disorder (social, obsessive or general anxiety)
May have low self-esteem
May have an additional diagnosis of bipolar disorder
If a visual thinker, can be overwhelmed by emotions; for example seeing a picture of an abused animal or person can be highly disturbing and she may not be able to remove the image(s) from her mind
May not understand her own emotions and those of others
May not know how to manage her emotions on her own
May not know how to comfort others

www.aspiengirl.com © Tania A. Marshall

A tendency to be clingy, have intense single friendships, not able to manage more than one friendship at a time

May be very shy *or* mute in social situations or may be on talk "overload" and not know when to stop talking

May have a special interest in a peer/hyperfocus on one friend, have a best friend

Feel more of a need or pressure/drive to be social

May float or flitter between groups at a superficial level

May play with younger or older children *or* prefer to talk to adults

Socially immature as compared to her peers

Less likely to have social difficulties that trigger a referral to a psychologist or psychiatrist, *until* teenage years

May lack an understanding of the social hierarchy, less understanding of the levels of friendship, including group roles and unwritten social rules

Have an ability to learn how to socialise and hide their difficulties, appearing to "blend in" more readily with their peer group (chameleon-like)

May have imaginary friends or imaginary pets as friends

Tends to observe and watch others, then mimic or copy them

May not apologise due to her need to be right and/or may be unaware that she has made a social mistake (depending on the situation)

May pretend she knows and/or understands the unwritten social rules when she does not

Social problems may not become apparent until tween or teen years, a much greater social impairment in early adolescence

More even profile of social skills until teenage years, where social difficulties become apparent

Can make friends and have conversations for short periods of time, however maintaining the friendship can be challenging

Desperate to please and appease others, may over-apologise or ask if someone is ok continuously, indicating she is unsure of the social rules

More likely to be enrolled in speech and drama lessons

May collect information on people

May observe and absorb the personality, speech, mannerisms, behaviours, lingo, clothing style, even rules and norms of an individual or group

A greater ability to use observation, imitation and masking in social situations, however the timing may be off. This may be referred to as chameleon-like, a "persona" or a façade. This can be seen by the copying of words, phrases, accents and/or sayings of other people and/or may be from books, television and/or movies

Play

May have difficulty sharing friendships, may be bossy (even aggressive) or passive, quiet and/or shy

Finds her peer's play confusing, boring or uninteresting. She may prefer to play on her own, with her animals/toys and/or with boys

Consists usually of complex set-ups, organising, sorting, collecting or grouping items rather than actually playing with them. She may be observed re-enacting a social scene from her own experiences at childcare/school

Spends more time setting up the scene, rather than playing with the parts of the scene

May follow other children around, not knowing what to do or how to engage socially

Can be obsessive with people

More ability to learn how to socialise and hide their difficulties, appear to "blend in" more readily with their peer group

Solitary play tends to include role-playing adults and/or using "scripts", learning how to act in social situations

Tend to use play and dolls to re-enact real-life social events

Tendency to interact mostly with younger children with whom she can direct the play

Non-Verbal Body Language

The appearance of extreme shyness or anxiety in girls may mask their lack of ability to understand social cues and/or their inability to be responsive to the social cues of others

A discrepancy between facial expression and feelings; for example, a "fake" smile and/or laugh, intense facial expressions or lack of, or inappropriate, facial expression to the situation

May wear a mask consisting of too much smiling or too serious much of the time

The 'resting face' is interpreted as angry or serious when the individual is usually deep in thought

A tendency to laugh, giggle and/or appear happy in serious situations, usually out of confusion as to how to respond or anxiety

Often can make appropriate eye contact; if not, it may appear as inconsistent or staring too long at people

Has difficulty understanding other people's nonverbal communication, facial expressions, tone of voice, appropriate distance and boundaries, body language, mind-reading and conversational skills

Communication/Speech and Language

May begin talking early or late

May have a loudness or softness in the voice, high pitch, monotone, hoarse or younger child-like quality

May be heard using a foreign accent

May have superior language skills

May have semantic pragmatic language challenges

May be mute at school, may avoid being asked a question by her teacher, may not ask for help and/or not know how to ask for help. May not occur to her to ask for help

May take language literally

May not know how to stand up for herself, say no and/or assert her needs and/or boundaries

May talk too much (talk overload)

May have repetitive motor movements or vocalisations that suggest a tic disorder

Developmental Milestones

May be ahead and behind in certain milestones (e.g. Hyperlexia)

May have talked early

More likely to be seen as "immature" socially and emotionally, yet above peers, e.g. in intelligence, reading ability

May have splinter skills doing some things very well and other things very poorly.

May have delays in self-help or self-care skills

May have delayed toileting

Interests

The interests are usually similar to their peers, however the *intensity* of them is noticeable. May have an interest(s) that are advanced and/or immature for her age, in comparison to her peers

Some common interests include: writing, reading, animals (horses, cats, dogs), stationery items, art, fantasy, anime, photography, music, languages, poetry, philosophy, psychology, technology and/or fashion

May show an interest very early on in understanding human behaviour. This may lead to have a career in the helping profession

www.aspiengirl.com © Tania A. Marshall

Self-Soothing Behaviours

May not have any repetitive behaviours or the behaviours are subtle and/or not representative of the 'male-based' repetitive behaviours. This may lead to a lack of diagnosis

Some repetitive behaviours include: chewing hair, biting nails, fiddling with fingers or objects, nail biting, twirling hair, wringing of the hands, picking fingers or skin, teeth grinding, toe wiggling, rubbing of one foot with the other, leg or foot-bouncing, swaying (whilst standing or sitting), fidgeting with hands, TMJ and/or throat-clearing or coughing (due to anxiety)

Usually less visible/noticeable than males

Tend to lack "male" repetitive and stereotyped behaviours, therefore leading to a lack of diagnosis

Sensory Sensitivities

May have problems ranging from sensitivities to intolerances to allergies

May be gluten, wheat, casein or lactose intolerant or allergic

May have eating issues and/or may not eat healthily and/or have an eating disorder

A tendency to eat mostly to only processed food

Sensory issues related to texture, the way food looks, foods mixed or touching each other

May have sensory sensitivities in the following areas: Visual, Hearing, Touch, Taste, Smell, Balance and Movement

May be an Empath and/or have a 6th Sense (knowing things without knowing how she knows them)

May take on others emotions as her own; may not be able to distinguish between her emotions and the emotions of other people

May have a special interest in food

May have Synaesthesia

Haircuts or hair brushing, brushing of teeth, trimming of nails and/or being touched may cause distress

May be overwhelmed by sensory input

May avoid working in large groups or being in noisy environments

May not feel pain, heat *or* cold or feel it too much

Fine and Gross Motor

May have an odd gait, walk on tippy toes, be clumsy and/or uncoordinated

May have handwriting or fine motor delays

May have difficulties knowing right from left

May avoid tasks that require hand-eye coordination or require the sequencing of complex movements

What to Look for in School

Generally well-behaved and quiet in the classroom and the opposite at home, a tendency

for parents of girls only to report that their daughters are having difficulties (including internalising problems) at home, with the teacher reporting no issues

Perfectionistic in her writing and/or work, has high expectations of herself and others

May appease and apologise too much, may not stand up for herself or assert boundaries

May make social faux pas, may be observed having social skills/theory of mind difficulties

May be on rule patrol and overly concerned with what others are doing or not doing

May appear to be 'off with the fairies'

May be selectively mute

May doodle on their books/paper

May appear to be highly sensitive, cry when frustrated, anxious or angry

Usually experiences intense emotional reactions and a high sense of justice. This can lead to a tendency to misinterpret and/or overreact and/or burn bridges

May look serious much of the time/may display emotions that do not match the situation

May be highly anxious about being called upon by the teacher

Usually has performance anxiety

May spend breaks by herself, walking the hallways, in the library, with a teacher or in the bathroom

May be the teacher's helper or the librarian's assistant

May avoid demands or complying with requests due to high anxiety levels

May complain of headaches and/or stomach aches

May have more school days off than her peers

May be bothered by lighting, or the set-up of the classroom (pictures on the walls, tables too close together, items hanging from the ceiling, chaotic presentation)

Tendency to be disorganised OR overly organised

Tendency to have difficulty with completion of tasks

May have a passive-aggressive nature

Usually high average to genius intelligence with learning differences/disability(s), may be a twice-exceptional child (gifted and Aspergers)

May tend to take others or the teacher literally

May not get others' jokes or sense of humour

www.aspiengirl.com © Tania A. Marshall

What to Look for in School

May have been diagnosed with ADHD, social anxiety, ODD or bi-polar disorder, and/or an eating disorder

Autism traits are hidden by learning difficulties, generalized anxiety and intense emotions or mood swings or often perceived as "shyness", social anxiety and/or bi-polar disorder

May be viewed as a little philosopher

Craves knowledge, loves to learn if she is interested in the topic, may prefer to teach herself rather than be taught

Self-Esteem and Identity

May have gender and/or sexuality confusion

May have low self-esteem

May lack a solid identity

May alter appearance to fit the group she is in at the time

May have several dramatic hair, clothing/appearance changes

Either not interested *or* overly interested in appearance

Can be careless *or* too interested in physical appearance and dress

May dress tom-boyish *or* ultra-princess like

May dress differently/unconventional for an occasion

Theory of Mind

Difficulty understanding that other people's thoughts are different from her own or that others cannot "know" certain things

Difficulty understanding non-verbal body communication and other people's perspectives

Difficulties with affective empathy, the ability to share another person's feelings with them. Often have too much empathy and compassion, and can tend to be overwhelmed by emotions

Context Blindness, a lack of awareness of the context as it relates to observation, learning, social interactions and communication

www.aspiengirl.com © Tania A. Marshall

Memory

Superior long-term memory

May have superior visual memory

A tendency to struggle with short-term memory

Imagination

Many have a very rich and elaborate fantasy world with detailed imaginary friends and/or imaginary animals, and at times difficulty distinguishing between reality and fantasy

Girls escape into fiction, and some live in another world with, for example, fairies, unicorns, witches and/or elves

Visual thinkers may be intensely involved with or caught up with a movie/book, leading them to feel and/or act like they are 'inside' the story. This can lead to trouble distinguishing between fantasy and reality

Cognitive Abilities

Executive function issues

May have slower processing speed

May have lower working memory

Typically average to genius intelligence (high functioning)

Lower working memory and/or processing speed

May have a split between verbal and perceptual intelligence

Tends to have cognitive profile consisting of high and low scores rather than average across the subscores

Sub-test scores tend to be a mixture of high to very high and low to very low

A tendency to fixate and hyperfocus on an area of interest

Some Talents, Gifts and Strengths

Intelligence

High creativity

Imaginative

Hyperempathy

Hyperfocus

Reading, writing, mathematics

Some Talents, Gifts and Strengths

Artistic endeavours (drawing, art, paining, photography, graphic design, anime)

Music (may have a perfect pitch and/or tone)

Languages (translating)

Performing arts (acting, singing and performing, dancing and modelling and/or fashion)

Highly intuitive

Hyperlexia

Determination

Self-taught learner

Introspection and curiosity

Idea generator

Obsession/High Interest in one or more areas/expert knowledge

Out-of-the-box thinker

Perfectionism

Skilled with animals, nature and children

Eye for detail

Editing and pointing out mistakes

Teaching others/presenting to others/performing

One-on-one interactions

Sense of humour

Truth-seeker/sense of justice

Technology

Some Learning Challenges or Conditions that Impact on Learning

May have:

Irlen Syndrome or Scotopic sensitivity

Dyslexia (reading difficulties)

Dysgraphia (writing difficulties)

Dyscalculia (mathematics difficulties)

Dyspraxia (motor planning difficulties)

Nonverbal learning disability (NLD)

Some Learning Challenges or Conditions that Impact on Learning

Auditory Processing Disorder

Lower Processing Speed

Lower Working Memory

Executive Function Issues

Weak Central Coherence

Some Commonly Observed Co-existing Conditions

ADHD/ADD

Eating disorder

Bi-polar

Alexythymia

Sensory Processing Disorder

Synaesthesia (a missing of the senses)

Irlen Syndrome

Anxiety Disorder

Depression

Sleep Disorder

Prosopagnosia (face blindness)

Pathological Demand Avoidance (PDA)

www.aspiengirl.com © Tania A. Marshall

Appendix 2
Ideas for Using AspienGirl®

The greatest gift an AspienGirl® can have is a diagnosis. For it is through the diagnosis that she gains knowledge and understanding of herself, of where she fits in the world, and her unique profile of characteristics, strengths and challenges. Discussing the diagnosis in a strengths-based way is crucial to her self-esteem and her future. Providing tools that address her weaknesses is also important.

Professionals:
This book is a great tool to use as a visual aid to help in explaining the unique profile of strengths and challenges and the diagnosis. I recommend explaining the diagnosis in a strengths-based way. You might like to utilise the pages in the book to point out to your client some of her strengths and challenges. Working together and creating an individualised strengths/challenges profile can be very useful, to not only the client, but also to her parents, family members and education staff. This profile can then be utilised in education planning meeting(s) with the teacher, teacher aide, guidance officer, school psychologist and/or other staff members involved.

1. With your client, go through the pages and discuss some of the strengths first, followed by some of the weaknesses or challenges. Make two separate lists on a whiteboard or on paper. Then discuss the unique profile in its entirety, introducing the terms Autism or Asperger Syndrome, the background/history of Autism/Asperger Syndrome.

2. After discussing your client's unique profile, having a conversation about successful female mentors who also have Autism or Asperger Syndrome can be a positive, hopeful and empowering next step. First, create and develop a list, including pictures, of females on the Spectrum and what they have achieved or are achieving. Second, explain to your client how the individual's unique profile and strengths may have contributed to them becoming a successful musician and/or having a successful career.

Parents/Family Members/Carers:
This book can be utilised as a great visual tool for girls who already have a diagnosis or those who may be self-diagnosing. This book can be used as an educational tool for siblings within

the family. Parents can use the book to explain their daughter's unique profile to siblings and/or extended family members. Parents may want to give a book to other family members or friends to help them gain awareness and understanding of female Autism. Using the visual pages to discuss some of the characteristics and how they are displayed or within the home, school or community environments can aid in awareness, understanding and tolerance.

Teachers/Educational Staff:
This book can be used as an educational tool for teachers and teacher aides, guidance officers, school psychologists and principals. This book can be used to gain awareness and understanding of females in the class or used as a means to teach and provide awareness to students in the classroom. The teacher can start the lesson by involving all the class in a discussion of strengths and weaknesses and bringing awareness that all people have inherent strengths and weaknesses. Children in the class can participate by volunteering their own strengths and/ or challenges profiles. A brief discussion of Autism, Asperger Syndrome and examples of well-known people on the Spectrum can also be helpful.

Appendix 3
Aspien*Girl*® Mentors

It is extremely important for AspienGirls to learn to view themselves through a strengths-based lens. You can help your client or daughter/grand-daughter/niece to research and learn more about girls/teens or female adults on the Autism Spectrum who are utilising their own personal strengths. The AspienGirl® and AspienWoman Mentor Interview Series was created to showcase the strengths, gifts and talents of females on the Spectrum. Interviews are being conducted and uploaded on a regular basis and are available at www.aspiengirl.com

You can help an AspienGirl® start their search by reading more about the following AspienGirls at www. aspiengirl.com/blog

On pages p141 - p.143:

Step 1: Read each AspienGirl® Mentor Interview at www.aspiengirl.com/blog

Step 2: Identify a strength(s) and a weakness(es) that the AspienGirl® discusses in her interview

Step 3: Record one or more strengths and weaknesses on the mentors page in this book

Step 4: For each mentor, think about what you like about that particular mentor and write it down on their page

Aspien*girl*® Mentors

Name: *Maja Nilsson*

Name: *Lydia Tay*

Name: *Honey Parker*

Aspien*girl*® Mentor

Name: *Maja Nilsson*

Interview with Maja Nilsson:
http://www.aspiengirl.com/blog/tag/Maja_Nilsson/

Strengths:

Challenges:

What I like about my AspienGirl® Mentor:

Aspien*girl*® Mentor

Name: Lydia Tay

Interview with Lydia Tay:
http://www.aspiengirl.com/blog/tag/Lydia_Tay/

http://aspergerjourney.blogspot.com.au/

Strengths:

Challenges:

What I like about my AspienGirl® Mentor:

Aspien*girl*® Mentor

Name: *Honey Parker*

Interview with Honey Parker:
http://www.aspiengirl.com/blog/tag/Honey_Parker/

Strengths:

Challenges:

What I like about my AspienGirl® Mentor:

Being My Own Superhero

WHAT I LIKE ABOUT ME

Name:

Find a photo or picture of yourself that you like and attach above. Write in your name underneath the picture.

Developing a list of personal strengths, talents and gifts is vital to healthy self-esteem and self-identity. Think of some qualities that you like about yourself and begin your list. Some examples might include intelligence, creativity or singing. You can look at the strengths list in Appendix I to help you. You can also ask your parents, relatives and/or friends to assist you. This list should be on-going, so keep adding to your list on a regular basis!

What I like about me

Appendix 4
BOYS VS. GIRLS

SOME RESEARCH-BASED AND CLINICAL ANECDOTAL GENDER DIFFERENCES
WWW.ASPIENGIRL.COM

Boys	Girls
Much of the research is based on males and male criteria and male assessment tools	Females are "research orphans", (Klin in Bazelon, 2007) Currently few female diagnostic assessment tools or screeners are available
A tendency to be louder and have their learning differences acknowledged in school	A tendency to be quiet and cooperative at school, not difficult to manage and therefore teachers may not be aware that they have difficulties. It may not be until females move to secondary school that the difficulties become more apparent
	Tendancy to be misdiagnosed (Nichols, Moravcik & Tetenbaum, 2008)
	Autism symptoms/difficulties are hidden by learning difficulties, anxiety and intense emotions or mood swings or perceived as "shyness" or social anxiety (Gould & Ashton-Smith, 2011)
Are identified by parents, professionals, teaching staff much earlier	Tend to be identified in the teenage years, or as an adult, if at all. Tend to be misdiagnosed
	Girls tend to manifest symptoms of Autism in subtle ways
Generally diagnosed earlier than girls	18 – 23% of adolescent girls with anorexia also present with signs of Autism/Asperger Syndrome. (Gillberg & Billstedt, 2000)
	A proportion of females with Autism may be overlooked or misdiagnosed because doctors see them first with anorexia (Auyeung & Baron-Cohen, 2013)
	Diagnosed later than boys; girls who receive a diagnosis of an Autistic Spectrum Condition (ASC) are generally more severe than boys with an ASC and more likely to be diagnosed with a learning difficulty, internalising disorder or eating disorder

Boys	Girls
Parents and teachers both tend to report behaviours and difficulties, both at school and at home	A tendency for parents of girls only to report that their daughters are having difficulties (including internalising problems and meltdowns), with the teacher reporting no issues; teachers often report very good to excellent behaviour at school
More likely to be disruptive and aggressive, in particular when stressed, frustrated or scared; tend to be described as active, angry	Rarely disruptive in the classroom, less hyperactive and impulsive

Less likely to have behaviours that trigger a referral to a psychologist or psychiatrist in the first place; tend to be described as anxious, depressed, passive or avoidant |
| **Greater social differences, uneven profile of social skills and experience social difficulties earlier** | May be socially interested and motivated, but unsuccessful in forming relationships with her peers or she may be able to make friends but have difficulty maintain the friendship

More socially appropriate (Head, McGillivray & Stokes, 2014) |
| **Less ability to fit in with peers and less pressure from society to be social** | Can make friends and have superficial conversations for short periods of time

More even profile of social skills until teenage years where social difficulties become very apparent; tendency to be more "socially" empathic |
| **Tends to lack a best friend** | More likely to have a best friend and follow other children around like a "shadow" (Kopp and Gillberg 2011) |
| **Boys demonstrating more social difficulties earlier in life** | More ability to learn how to socialise and hide their difficulties, appear to "blend in" more readily with their peer group; better adaptation/compensation in girls (Dworzynski, K., Ronald, A., Bolton, P. & Happé, F., 2012); feel more of a need or pressure/drive to be social; may have just one special friend

A tendency to follow their peers in social interactions with greater ability to use observation, imitation and masking in social situations, however the social timing may be off. This may be referred to as chameleon-like, a "persona" or a façade (Attwood, 2006)

Tendency to interact mostly with younger children (Kopp & Gillberg, 2011), can connect with younger children who will allow them to set the terms of play

May gravitate towards older children/teens |

Boys	Girls
A tendency for noticeable lack of eye contact	Tend to make eye contact or have more eye contact or too much eye contact (stare)
More likely to be seen as "odd" or "viewed as a little professor" by peers	More likely to be seen as "immature" and/or a "little philosopher"
More likely to externalise their anger, frustration or stress, tend to be more aggressive and domineering and strong desire for sameness	More likely to internalise or cry a lot, maybe mute and/or shy, the traits of ASC can appear as extreme shyness or anxiety in girls, masking that they may not be responsive to the social cues of others More passive aggressive More likely to avoid demands (Kopp and Gillberg 2011) or have traits of PDA (Pathological Demand Avoidance)
Can be obsessive with people, but usually in more direct ways	Can be obsessive with people, usually in indirect or passive aggressive ways
More likely to have language problems	Language problems are less likely The tendency to have superior language abilities; better communication skills and more advanced social skills hides their challenges
	More likely to be clingy and have separation anxiety issues; young girls with Autism have been found to appear more anxious and depressed
More noticeable repetitive motor movements, attention and communication problems	Less to no repetitive movements, disruptive or communication issues. Communication more likely to be expressed as silence or muteness
More features of restricted interests and more characteristics of repetitive behaviours More repetitive behaviours such as rocking or spinning	Less to no repetitive behaviours; may miss being diagnosed due to a "lack of repetitive and stereotyped behaviours". Overall, girls may show less repetitive stereotyped behaviour than boys (Mandy, Chilvers, Chowdhury, Salter, Siegel & Skuse, 2012)

Boys	Girls
Special interests include (for example): dinosaurs, trains, cars, technology, technical hobbies and facts	Special interests are similar to their female peers, however are much more intense; it is the quality and intensity of the interests that are different Interests are less object-related Some of these interests include fairies, unicorns, dragons, fantasy, celebrities, animals, nature or a sport Sort, group, catalogue or place their toys rather than "lining up" (Kopp & Gillberg, 2011)
A tendency to be less imaginative in play	More imagination and the pretend play is better (Knickmeyer, Wheelwright, & Baron-Cohen, 2008), often interested in imaginative play and sometimes obsessively Very good imagination includes imaginary friends, games, being animals or taking on the persona of other girls Many have a very rich and elaborate fantasy world with imaginary friends. Girls escape into fiction, and some live in another world with, for example, fairies and witches Solitary play tends to include role-playing adults and/or using "scripts", learning how to act in social situations, a tendency to use play and dolls to re-enact real-life social events Pretend or imaginary friends/animals and at times trouble distinguishing between reality and fantasy
Tendency to act out or externalise in order to avoid or ignore demands	A tendency to be more passive and avoidant, due to high anxiety. More likely to avoid demands Girls may be more likely to avoid demands passively, by ignoring them, rather than acting out like boys (Kopp & Gillberg, 2011) Highly intuitive and hyper-empathic; many females report knowing things without knowing how they know them, not being able to watch horror, violence, the news, animals being hurt or misused

Boys	Girls
A tendency to interrupt, be too loud or miss the point or context of a situation	A tendency to be silent (too quiet)
	A tendency to pretend she "gets" a joke or know what's going on in the conversation, rather than risk criticism, conflict or ridicule
	Either not interested or overly-interested in appearance (Kopp & Gillberg, 2011)
Voice: A monotone or "robot-like" voice is considered fairly typical of boys with Asperger's or high-functioning Autism while males excel in visuo-spatial tasks (Wing, 1981)	Voice: instead, the girls were more likely to speak in a high-pitched, childish or hoarse voice (Kopp and Gilberg, 2011)
	Females have better verbal skills (Wing, 1981)
More likely to have attention-deficit/hyperactivity disorder	Girls tend to be less hyperactive, less distractible than boys, and more able to focus, making them instead appear as if they're daydreaming.
	Girls with high verbal IQ were less likely to have social communication problems; higher verbal IQ may gave girls a protective factor against social communication problems
	As assessed on diagnostic instruments for Autism, the communicative abilities of girls with ASC have been observed to be stronger (e.g. pointing, gaze following)
Boys with ASC may tend to engage in disruptive behaviour to gain objects	Girls with ASC may tend to engage in disruptive behaviour to get attention
Collects information on objects	Collects information on people; may show an interest very early on in understanding human behaviour. This may lead to have a career in the helping profession
Tendency towards factual books	Tendency towards a love of reading poetry and fantasy; escaping into fiction and imaginary friends

*** Different age groups may show different levels of skills and impairments

*** A general summary of the above-referenced research. Specific findings may vary depending on the age, level of intellectual ability, observed or parent report measures on skills and behaviours and the type of sample (lab or clinic) being researched.

References

Attwood, T. (2006) *The pattern of abilities and development for girls with Asperger's Syndrome.* In Asperger's and Girls. Eds. Arlington, TX: Future Horizons Inc.

Baron-Cohen S., Jaffa, T., Davies, S., Auyeung, B., Allison, C., and Wheelwright, S. (2013) "Do girls with anorexia nervosa have elevated Autistic traits?" *Molecular Autism* 2013, 4:24.

Bazelon, E. (2007) "What Autistic girls are made of ." *The New York Times Magazine*, August 5, 2007. Available at www.nytimes.com/2007/08/05/magazine/05autism-t.html, accessed on May 2nd, 2014.

Dworzynski, K., Ronald, A., Bolton, P. and Happé, F. (2012) "How different are girls and boys above and below the diagnostic threshold for Autism spectrum disorders?" *Journal of the American Academy of Child and Adolescent Psychiatry* 51, 788-797.

Gillberg, C. and Billstedt, E. (2000) "Autism and Asperger syndrome: Coexistence with other clinical disorders." *Acta Psychiatria Scandinavica* 102, 321–330.

Gould, J. and Ashton-Smith, J. (2011) "Missed diagnosis or misdiagnosis: girls and women on the autism spectrum." *Good Autism Practice* 12, 1, 34-41.

Head, A., McGillivray, J.A., and Stokes, M.A. (2014) "Gender differences in emotionality and sociability in children with Autism spectrum disorders." *Molecular Autism* 2014, 5:19.

Knickmeyer, R. C., Wheelwright, S., and Baron-Cohen, S. B. (2008) "Sex typical play: Masculinization/defeminization in girls with an Autism spectrum condition." *Journal of Autism and Developmental Disorders* 38, 6, 1028-1035.

Kopp, S. and Gillberg, C. (2011) "The Autism Spectrum Screening Questionnaire (ASSQ) - Revised Extended Version (ASSQ-REV): An instrument for better capturing the Autism phenotype in girls?" *Research in Developmental Disabilities 32*, 6, 2875-88.

Mandy, W., Chilvers, R., Chowdhury, U., Salter, G. et al. (2012) "Sex differences in Autism spectrum disorder: Evidence from a large sample of children and adolescents." *Journal of Autism and Developmental Disorders 42*, 7, 1304-1313.

Nichols, S., Moravcik, G., & Tetenbaum, S. P. (2008) *Girls growing up on the Autism spectrum: What parents and professionals should know about the pre-teen and teenage years.* London: Jessica Kingsley Publishers.

Wing, L. (1981) "Sex ratios in early childhood autism and related conditions." *Psychiatry Research*, 5, 129-37.

Further Projects

The AspienGirl® and AspienWoman Mentor Project and Interview Series was created due to the lack of information about successful females on the Spectrum and their innate strengths. I have been privileged to meet females of all ages with a stunning array of AspienPowers (gifts, talents, strengths and/or abilities, strengths unique to females, yes, and males, but I am writing about females here) who are true warriors, heroines, and superheroes. These women have all overcome challenges and continue to shine a light for themselves and others. This is what makes them a warrior.

I am in the process of gathering interviews of females on the Spectrum, of all ages, from all over the world who are excellent role models, mentors, heroines and superheroes, who have unique talents and strengths, and who provide inspiration and hope to others on the Spectrum. Current interviews can be viewed on my blog at www.aspiengirl.com/blog

If you or someone you know would like to be a Mentor for others by showcasing your talents, success, abilities, please contact me at tania@aspiengirl.com

The **AspienGirl® Project** was created to address several issues:

Awareness: Females have Autism or Aspergers, are often misdiagnosed and receiving inappropriate interventions.

Advocacy: Females are marginalized members of society. AspienGirls form a minority sub-culture within this larger marginalized group of females, and as such, have unique needs and challenges.

Education: There is little knowledge of Aspiengirls around the world. An important step is to make available resources about the female profile across the lifespan, gender differences, interventions and support for females, in as many languages and countries as possible.

Philanthropy: AspienGirls seeking a diagnosis are often not able to afford the cost. The AspienGirl® Project will donate a percentage of book sales to cover the costs of diagnoses for those that cannot afford it.

Future Titles

What traits and gifts make this group of women so unique and often misunderstood? I Am AspienWoman helps those with or those working with Asperger Syndrome or Autism by using a strengths-based approach to introduce the unique **adult** female profile of characteristics, traits and gifts.

Tania Marshall, M.Sc. is releasing this book to fill a massive gap in the market. Working daily in private practice there just wasn't an appropriate female resource to share. Clients were requesting for resources specifically written for them.

If you are looking a book on the adult female Autism Spectrum traits, then this is the perfect book for you.

Using positive strengths-based language, Tania Marshall showcases the gifts and talents of the many females that she has personally worked with. If you have been searching for a book that describes what Aspiens CAN do, can accomplish, and can BE, then this is the book for you. This book provides hope for any AspienGirl's future, by discussing and focusing on the unique combination of talents, strengths and gifts commonly seen in individuals with Asperger Syndrome or Autism. This book is focused on what this remarkable group of females can do and the positive future they can have, once they focus on their strengths.

Releasing soon in French, Italian, Spanish, Norwegian, German, Hungarian, Dutch, Chinese and Brazilian Portuguese.

About the Author

Tania Marshall is a psychologist and author with 20 years of experience in the field of child and family psychology, Autism, Asperger Syndrome and related conditions, giftedness, Twice-Exceptional, Genius and Savant Syndrome and highly sensitive individuals.

She is currently working on her Doctoral Degree, with a specialisation in Autism Studies, in particular Female Asperger Syndrome. She currently divides her time between private practice, diagnostic assessments, post-diagnosis support, intervention, writing and research.

Please go to www.aspiengirl.com and make sure you sign up for our newsletter. You can also stay up-to-date with the book series, The AspienGirl® and AspienWoman Mentor Project and Interview Series, The AspienGirl® Project Webinar Series, tips, resources, blogs, and more! To contact Tania for assessments, workshops, presentations, book signings or remote Skype consulting, please email her at tania@aspiengirl.com

For more information:
W: www.taniamarshall.com
W: www.aspiengirl.com
T: www.twitter.com/TaniaAMarshall
T: www.twitter.com/aspiengirlVIP
FB: www.facebook.com/taniamarshallauthor
FB: www.facebook.com/aspiengirl
Pinterest: https://pinterest.com/taniaamarshall
Wordpress: www.aspiengirl.com/blog
LinkedIn: au.linkedin.com/in/taniaannmarshall/

Notes

CPSIA information can be obtained
at www.ICGtesting.com
Printed in the USA
LVHW060215180419
614631LV00003B/27/P

9 780992 360900